PRESENTING

BREWED
with
BALLS

AFFIRM press

Published by Affirm Press in 2016
28 Thistlethwaite Street, South Melbourne, VIC 3205.
www.affirmpress.com.au

National Library of Australia Cataloguing-in-Publication entry available for this title.
Title: Brewed with Balls / Stephanie Bishop-Hall, author.
ISBN: 9781925344622 (paperback)

Cover and book design by Karen Wallis
Illustration by Karen Wallis
Cover image artjazz/Shutterstock.com

Printed in China by 1010 Printing
All images credited to the breweries unless otherwise stated.

PRESENTING

BREWED *with* BALLS

THE MOST OUTLANDISH BEERS ON THE PLANET

introduction by

JOSH ULJANS & KARL VAN BUUREN
FROM MOON DOG CRAFT BREWERY

AFFIRM press

INTRODUCTION *by*

JOSH ULJANS AND KARL VAN BUUREN
co-founders of Moon Dog Craft Brewery

BEER IS MANY THINGS TO MANY PEOPLE. IT'S DELICIOUS, EXCITING, ENTHRALLING AND REFRESHING, BUT most of all it's fun. Five years ago, we decided that we loved beer so much that we should start our own brewery. Not just any old brewery, mind you; we wanted to create truly wondrous beers, like no beer ever brewed before. We wanted to take our drinkers on a sensory journey of discovery and intrigue, experiencing flavours in a glass that they'd never thought possible. The humble drink of the people would be re-imagined into something really freaking innovative and cool. And when people were drinking our beers, they would be thinking, "Fuck! This is delicious and fun!" *Brewed with Balls* cracks open this spirit of fun and adventure that's pushing beer and beer-makers to heady new heights.

The eternally wise Google tells us that beer is, 'an alcoholic drink made from yeast-fermented malt, flavoured with hops.' (As brewers, we should probably already know that.) From four simple ingredients – malt, hops, water and yeast – the most amazingly diverse and delicious flavours can be produced. Delicate, floral pilseners; hearty stouts with flavours of coffee and chocolate; ball-tearingly bitter IPAs; and funky Belgian sours with flavours akin to 'wet horse blanket': the flavours and aromas that a talented brewer can produce in beer are limitless. The skill of the brewer is demonstrable in the balance of their brewed beverage – a harmonious symphony of flavours to be gleefully guzzled from a pint glass.

Being the Gen Y jerks we are, we wanted to do something different. The four basic ingredients of beer can be augmented with other cool ingredients and made into something really fucking tasty.

Ingredients like, say, Tasmanian black truffles. Why? Because it's fun, and they are delicious. Or cherry plums? Also fun and delicious. Or making two beers that are designed to be blended together in the one glass, and when you do the combination tastes like an Old Fashioned cocktail? Fucking delicious. Fucking fun.

Brewers all over the world are becoming increasingly experimental. Pioneers of what some have dubbed 'extreme beer' – what we consider to be the 'pointy end' of innovation in craft beer – such as Rogue Ales in Oregon or Jester King in Texas, have been challenging perceptions of beer for yonks. But flick through the history books and you'll see that beers even thousands of years ago had some pretty weird shit going on. The common thread that ties brewers of interesting brews together is that we LOVE making these types of beers. We love the science, the challenge, the risk (not all out-there beers make the cut ...) and the reward of having produced something great that's unlike anything made before.

There's a bit of a difference between making a really enjoyable, interesting and unique beer, and jamming some shit into a beer to create a headline-grabbing novelty. As much as some of the ingredients we use are novel, everything we put in our beers has a purpose. It's well thought out. It's there because it adds to the deliciousness of the beer, and integrates well with the other flavours. The balance of flavours still has to be there for the beer to work, and that's pretty bloody hard when you're using weird and wonderful extra ingredients! We reckon you can put anything into a beer, as long as it tastes good.

When we're conceptualising, designing, brewing, packaging and finally drinking the beers, we've got big, stupid smiles on our faces. Although, those smiles have, on occasion, morphed into pensive puzzlement as we ponder the quandary of removing 300 kilograms of soggy gingerbread from a fermentation tank. More than anything, though, we make these beers because we know you'll love them and we want you to have that big, stupid smile on your face too.

This book takes you on a journey through some of the most innovative and out-there beers on the planet, made by passionate brewers like us for beer lovers like you because we know you'll get a big kick out of drinking them. Cheers!

Josh & Karl

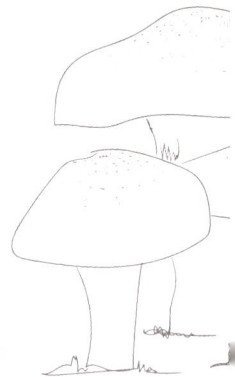

JESTER KING BREWERY

SNÖRKEL

SALT IS GREAT, MUSHROOMS ARE GREAT, AND SO JESTER

King had a pretty great idea and added them together to make a great brew. They gave their neighbours at Logro Farms some used grain from their other brews to grow the mushies in, and then, when it came time to start fermentation, they added regular sea salt and smoked sea salt to ensure that serious flavour hit. And Snörkel was born. It's a farmhouse-style ale with a lemony, earthy taste. The mushrooms inform the earthy flavour that's desirable in a farmhouse ale, without actually making it taste like a mushroom. We'll let you decide if that's a good thing or not.

SHORT'S BREWING COMPANY

KEY LIME PIE

KEY LIME PIES MAY BE AN AMERICAN SPECIALTY, BUT there is no reason that this sweet and tangy treat shouldn't be embraced by the rest of the world (just find a picture of one and we're sure you'll agree). And perhaps the best way to get acquainted with this delicious pie is through a beer. Not just any beer, though: a beer brewed with fresh limes, milk sugar, marshmallow fluff and even biscuits to give that essential crust flavour. Short's Key Lime Pie beer begins immensely sweet and then turns tart, just like the real thing. Mmm.

Making a cake or a beer? Curt Guntzviller brewing the Key Lime Pie.

SAPPORO

SPACE BARLEY

FOR THIS WACKY BREW, JAPANESE AND RUSSIAN SCIENTISTS got together and tested how well barley could grow in space, planting barley seeds on the Zvezda Service Module of the International Space Station. (Isn't it nice to see international cooperation on world-changing projects?) After spending five months in orbit, and actually growing, the barley was brought back to earth so that the Russian Academy of Sciences, Okayama University and Sapporo could work together to brew the world's first 'space beer'. Prices were pretty out of this world – sixpacks of the space beer were sold in a lottery system for over a hundred dollars each. Researchers apparently said the beer tasted no different to that containing Earth-grown barley, but at least you'd be able to say you'd drunk alien beer.

MOON DOG
CRAFT BREWERY

OGDEN NASH'S
PASH RASH

IMAGINE LANDING YOUR DREAM JOB IN A BREWERY AND getting the chance to learn the mysterious alchemy of the brew ... but instead the bossman points you towards a pile of 5800 Redskin lollies and tells you to unwrap the lot. Well, as you chuck the lollies one by one into the vat, you can rest assured that it's for a worthy cause – namely Ogden Nash's Pash Rash. It's an imperial Redskin stout from Moon Dog, one of Australia's most experimental breweries, and it has a massive candied raspberry aroma that will send your nostalgia receptors into sweet overdrive. The dark chocolate and coffee flavours of the stout work exceedingly well with the raspberry of the Redskins, making the Pash Rash much, much more than just a novelty brew.

THE UNITED STATES

by

DOCK STREET BREWERY

AIN'T NOTHING TO FUNK WITH

DOCK STREET BREWERY RELEASED AIN'T NOTHING TO FUNK WITH at the end of 2015: a golden saison barrel-aged to the music of Wu-Tang Clan. Custom-made headphones were fitted to the barrel, and the grungy East Coast beats of Wu-Tang played on a loop 24/7 for six months. The brewers say they wanted to know how other factors would influence the beer – not just obvious ones like temperature and light exposure, but 'rhythm, tempo and volume' too. The beer had a limited release, sold out in record time and was launched by Inspectah Deck of Wu-Tang Clan spinning his group's classics at the brewery. Although most people would probably go nuts if put through the same treatment, let's hope a little piece of the genius of Wu-Tang Clan seeped into Dock Street's golden saison.

DOCK STREET BEER

BORG BRUGGHÚS

FENRIR NR. 26

FENRIR NR. 26 FROM ICELAND IS A SMOKED IPA. A SHEEP shit smoked IPA. Yes indeed, the boys from Borg Brugghús tell us that using the smoke from burning sheep poo to smoke the malts not only creates a unique and wonderful flavour but is also an Icelandic tradition. Perhaps because of the lack of trees in Iceland, using sheep poo to smoke lamb and fish has been a thing for centuries. The smoke from the sheep poo is heavier than boring old wood smoke and brings a 'farmish' or 'country' aroma to the party (we'll let you interpret that how you will). With this particular beer, though, the heaviness of the poo smoke is balanced out by the hoppiness of the IPA. So there you go. Let's just be straight-up and say Iceland is a weird and wonderful place.

Borg Brugghús Brewer Sturlaugur Jón Björnsson and horse.

NAIL BREWING

ANTARCTIC NAIL ALE

HEAD BREWER AND OWNER OF NAIL BREWING, JOHN Stallwood, has a brother-in-law who used to volunteer for the Sea Shepherd marine conservation organisation. While on a trip down to Antarctica with the famous seafaring environmentalists, John's brother from another mother decided to chip off a sneaky chunk of iceberg and take it home as a souvenir. The ice travelled all the way to Tasmania, before crossing the country and arriving in Perth safe and sound – if rather more watery. That water was used in brewing thirty bottles of Antarctic Nail Ale. This classic Australian-style pale ale was then auctioned off by the bottle and sold for over $800 Aussie dollars each. One even went for a whopping $1850! All proceeds went to the Sea Shepherd and their whale conservation programs.

BREWDOG

THE END OF HISTORY

THIS BEER IS A RIPPER. BREWDOG'S THE END OF HISTORY IS outrageous in every possible way. It's named after philosopher Francis Fukuyama's famous work, in which he defined 'history' as the evolution of the political system through the ages. For Fukuyama, humanity had reached the end of its political evolution, and consequently it was 'the end of history'. Now, in Brewdog's own words, their rodent-encased beverage 'is to beer what democracy is to history'. It's over, everyone go home: the boundaries of extreme brewing have been pushed as far as they'll go. The End of History is a blonde Belgian ale infused with nettles from the Scottish Highlands and fresh juniper berries, and it's a whopping 55 per cent ABV. Only twelve bottles were made, each sold with a certificate of authenticity, and packaged in a stuffed stoat or squirrel. These are real animals, though the brewery assures us they were all roadkill first.

BREWMEISTER

SNAKE VENOM

SCOTLAND'S BREWMEISTER CLAIMS THE TITLE OF 'WORLD'S most alcoholic beer' with Snake Venom. This brew is a massive 67.5 per cent alcohol (so it probably does have a similar effect on the body to snake venom ...), well above the usual ABV of 4 to 8 per cent. Traditional brewing alone won't create an alcohol content that big, so brewers use a technique called 'fractional freezing'. It involves keeping the beer very cold and removing the chunks of ice that form (since alcohol takes an extremely low temperature to freeze, these chunks contain nothing but water), which concentrates the beer bit by bit. Anyway, the final product is even stronger than many hard liquors – whiskey, for example, is usually around 40 per cent alcohol. So, we guess you could sip it slowly or shot it with a slice of lemon? Every bottle comes with a warning tag wrapped around its neck with a gentle reminder not to drink too much. And we would definitely take that advice.

Snake Venom being brewed.

NAIL BREWING

FLAMING LAMINGTON

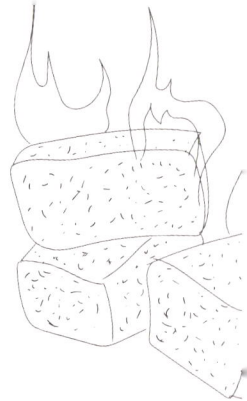

THE FLAMING LAMINGTON BEER HAS MORE THAN JUST A great name. It is a chocolate stout brewed with 80 kilograms of baked coconut and 25 kilograms of chillies. Nothing could be more Australian than combining lamingtons and beer, but to add that hit of chilli is a stroke of genius – it makes this drink the alcoholic equivalent of your great auntie cutting loose on 'Mexican Night' at the local. To achieve that flavour, the brewers had to lower the chillies and the stout grains into the fermenter in huge tea bags and then pull them out again, like a giant making a cup of chilli tea. This stout, which starts off creamy and rich but leaves behind a whiff of spicy heat, has been so popular it is now brewed annually. It would do Alf Stewart proud.

ROGUE ALES

THE BEARD BEER

LOCATED IN OREGON IN THE US, A PLACE OVERFLOWING with both beer and beards, Rogue is a brewery staffed by passionate people who really pour themselves into their work. And we mean that quite literally. The Beard Beer is an American wild ale that's made with yeast found on the hairs of brewmaster John Maier's beard. Can we just pause for a moment and think about that – beard yeast. Yeast created from a dude's hair. Rogue assured us that John has had the same beard since the late 1970s (not quite sure how that's reassuring, though). The beer has been described as 'spicy' and may even put hairs on your chest (or face).

Rogue's brewmaster John Maier.

SHORT'S BREWING COMPANY

SPRUCE PILSNER

TO THE UNTRAINED EYE, THE PICEA PUNGENS, OR BLUE spruce tree, looks very much like a traditional European Christmas tree – all it needs is a star on top and a fat man with a beard loitering around. However, this spiky fellow is actually native to North America, and the Short's brewing team like it so much that they hand-pick its prickly needles for their Spruce Pilsner. They are so protective of these needles that they source them from a secret location near the brewery in Michigan. The spruce tips give the pilsner a 'refreshing gin quality', which is one of the most appealing beer descriptions we've ever heard. Short's tells us that their spruce use is inspired by historical brewing practices, so even ye olde types didn't mind a dash of tree in their beverage. And if it's good enough for the beer buffs of yesteryear, it's darn well good enough for us.

Joe Short with some handpicked secret spruce.

MOON DOG
CRAFT BREWERY

MR MISTOFFELEES

YOU MIGHT REMEMBER MR MISTOFFELEES AS THAT SINGING and dancing cat from that musical about cats called *Cats*. Well, this passionfruit and mango blonde wild ale has just as much pizzazz as a lycra-clad feline doing a somersault. Like many experimental beers, it's aged in barrels inoculated with impressive-sounding wild yeast cultures (*Brettanomyces* and *lactobacillus*, just to name a couple), and these micro-organisms change the flavours of the beer to create the distinctive earthy and sour characters that people love (or hate) in wild ales. The folk at Moon Dog add passionfruit and mango to the barrels before leaving the yeast to do its thing for a whole six months. The result is a brew with strong tropical flavours – the bottled embodiment of a cat with jazz hands.

Moon Dog brewery.

THE UNITED STATES
by

RIGHT BRAIN BREWERY

MANGALITSA PIG PORTER

RIGHT BRAIN BREWERY DESCRIBES THIS BEER AS the one that put them on the map. It's a big, rich porter with chocolatey flavours and it's brewed with pigs' heads and bones. It's a porky porter, you could say. Poor old Babe. The porter is reportedly very delicious and the brewery describes it is as a similar experience to wrapping a big pretzel in a slice of ham and dipping it in chocolate. Sounds good – if not ridiculously indulgent and heart-attack inducing.

4 PINES BREWING COMPANY

VOSTOK CERTIFIED SPACE BEER

AUSTRALIA'S OWN 4 PINES CLAIMS THE HONOUR OF BREWING the first-ever beer that can be consumed in space. In a deal with Saber Astronautics, 4 Pines set out to find a solution to the age-old problem of how to open and drink a beer in zero gravity without it exploding all over the place. This entailed a number of tests, including a drop tower test – dropping the beer off a tall tower to simulate the effect of zero gravity – and then microgravity testing involving the 'vomit comet', a zero-gravity flight on which the beer was first served. The result was the Vostok. The low carbonation and concentrated flavours of this dry Irish stout, as well as the specially designed bottle, apparently allow it to be opened and consumed in zero gravity. But never fear, you don't have to be an astronaut to enjoy the Vostok – you can drink a bottle right here on Earth … It just might not be quite as fun.

4 Pines brewer Garrett at the Brookvale Brewery.

MIKKELLER

BEER GEEK BRUNCH WEASEL

THIS IMPERIAL OATMEAL STOUT IS BREWED WITH ONE OF the world's most expensive coffees: weasel poo coffee (more formally known as 'kopi luwak'). The coffee beans are eaten by the very fussy South-East Asian civet cat, which looks something like a large, weird cat–weasel beast thing. The civets only eat the best and ripest coffee berries, and their digestive systems (apparently) help to break down the beans and enhance their flavours. In one of the more glamourous jobs in the coffee industry, workers collect the droppings and 'clean' the coffee beans before preparing them for sale. Civet coffee is very rare and has a really strong taste and aroma. So, weasel poo aside, in Mikkeller's brew, this adds a super-rich roasted coffee flavour to the characteristic smooth sweetness of the oatmeal stout. It's like brunch in a bottle.

by

ABASHIRI

BILK

BEER + MILK = BILK. HERE'S WHY: WHEN LIQUOR STORE owner Chitoshi Nakahara felt bad about surplus milk getting wasted in Nakashibetsu, Japan's biggest dairy farming region, he got thinking. He suggested the idea of using the milk in a beer to local brewery Abashiri, and Bilk was born. Unlike the traditional milk stout, which is made with only a small amount of lactose to add some creamy sweetness, this interesting brew is made with a whole 30 per cent milk along with 70 per cent regular beer. (Mmm, can you feel it curdling in your stomach yet?) Apparently the production process doesn't differ that much from regular beer, and it tastes quite similar to normal beer too. It's fruity and sweet and a bit creamy looking. And if you're not disgusted by the whole concept then you might just love it.

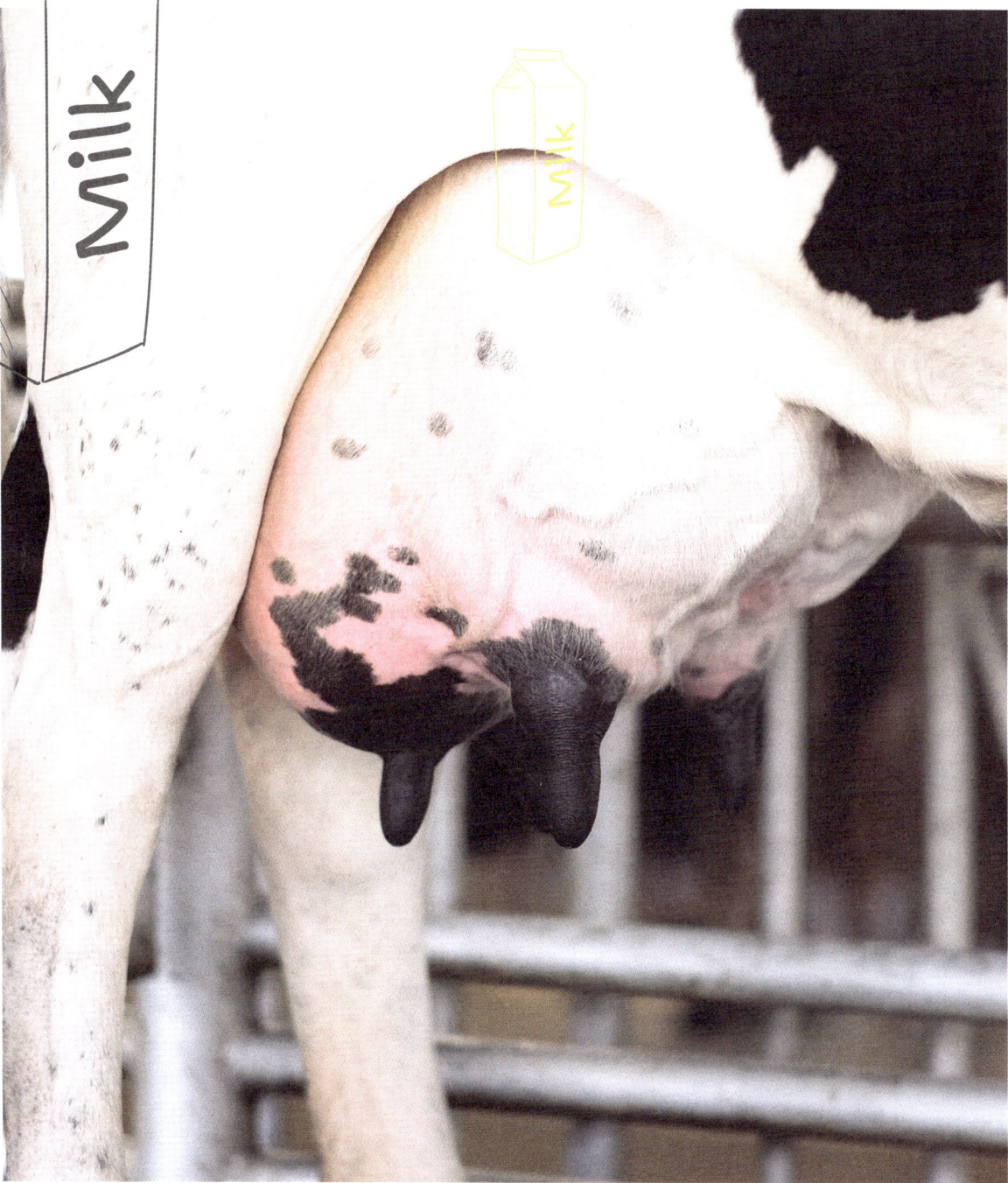

JESTER KING BREWERY

EQUIPOISE

ONE OF MANY WACKY BREWS MADE IN COLLABORATION with a chef, Equipose is brewed with ginger salt and tarragon and then refermented with cantaloupe. Take a moment to think about those flavours. Cantaloupe, tarragon and ginger salt all blended together in a farmhouse ale. A perfect combination – like orange and chocolate, or Kim and Kanye. Equipoise has complex flavours to match its complex make-up, and should be served in a minimalist dining room by a waiter with a manic smile and a white napkin over their arm.

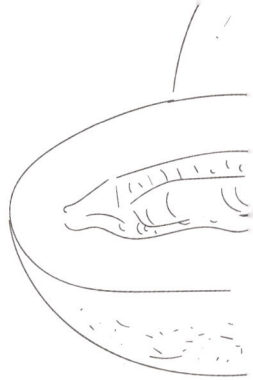

AUSTRALIA
by
MATSO'S BROOME BREWERY
CHILLI BEER

HERE'S ONE THAT'LL BLOW YOUR HEAD OFF – MATSO'S Chilli Beer is one hot drop. It's brewed as a wheat beer with wheat and pilsner malts, and fermented with an ale yeast to give it a spicy clove character. Head brewer Dave describes the secret super chilli oil as being 'ruthlessly infused' into the beer. He adds that Matso wants to see you 'cry for your mamma'. Originally made for the Fremantle Chilli Festival and bottled for the first time in 2013, Chilli Beer can also be diluted following the recipes in 'Matso's Mixery'. These recipes, created for those who can't hack the heat or who want a flavour twist, combine Chilli Beer with some of Matso's other favourites: their alcoholic Ginger Beer (creating an 'Angry Ranga'), Mango Beer (Chango), Bishop's Beer (Angry Bishop) and Lychee Beer (Lychilli). Choose your poison …

by

BRUGGHÚS STEÐJA

HVALUR 2

HVALUR MEANS 'WHALE' IN ICELANDIC, SO THAT'S A BIT OF a hint as to what this beer involves. Hvalur 2 is brewed for the month of Thorri (*Þorri*, the fourth month of winter in Iceland, which has ancient sacred significance). During Thorri, Icelanders keep out the chill with traditional foods such as ram's testicles, rotten shark and soured whale fat. And don't we just wish we could be there to experience it. For Hvalur 2, the brewers get fresh whale testicles from a fin whale and smoke them with that old Icelandic favourite: sheep poo. Each brew contains one testi that weighs around eight kilograms. The sheep poo brings its heavy smoke flavours to the beer, while the testicles bring a 'meaty, whaley taste'. Yum. The brewers explain they wanted to instil this beer with the atmosphere of Thorri, and they think they have created the perfect *Þorrabjór* (beer for Thorri).

by

WYNKOOP BREWING COMPANY

ROCKY MOUNTAIN OYSTER STOUT

THE TITLE HERE IS MISLEADING. NO OYSTERS IN THIS STOUT – at least, not the ones you're thinking of. Only the usual barley, yeast, some more barley, a few hops and 12 kilograms of thinly sliced and roasted bull testicles (three per barrel, to be precise). Confused? Well, in Colorado cowboy talk, bull's testicles are known as 'Rocky Mountain Oysters'. This beer supposedly started as an April Fool's joke that went a bit too far. The brewers at Wynkoop created a foreign-style stout with the Rocky Mountain Oysters for a bit of a laugh, but the beer was so good they had to keep making it. It's got the big chocolatey flavours and high alcohol of a foreign stout, plus a bit of a savoury note that may or may not be thanks to the ball content. Whatever the case, it's a beer that really hits you where it hurts.

Wynkoop
BREWING COMPANY

ROCKY MOUNTAIN
OYSTER STOUT

STOUT BREWED WITH BULL TESTICLES

WYNKOOP'S

EVEN
SMALLER
BATCH

SERIES

WYNKOOP
BREWING COMPANY

ROCKY MOUNTAIN OYSTER STOUT

STOUT BREWED WITH BULL TESTICLES

WYNKOOP'S

EVEN SMALLER BATCH

SERIES

12 FL OZ (355 ML)   7.5% ALC. BY VOL.

Yes. that is an actual bull's testicle.

RED DUCK

RA#3

RED DUCK'S RA#3 IS AN EGYPTIAN BREAD BEER, AND IT'S more feral than a Tantanoola tiger. Red Duck asserts that their creation is entirely unlike any other beer, describing it as 'funky, sour and spiced up'. The yeast used in this beer is like runny sourdough starter (hence the 'bread' part). The flavours added come from classic North African ingredients, such as coriander pods, ginger, cinnamon, nutmeg, apricots, sultanas, orange peel and za'atar spice mix (hence the 'Egyptian'). There are no hops in this one, just heaps of mashed grains, and it looks similar to champagne but tastes intensely spicy and sour like a kick in the tongue. RA#3's loving creators have called their baby 'a freaking beautiful freak', but they assure their customers that only 960 bottles of the brew will be created, just in case it gets out of its enclosure and starts attacking the native wildlife.

Red Duck brewery.

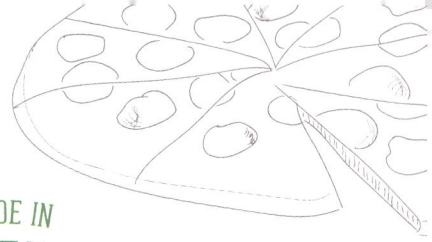

THE UNITED STATES
by

MAMMA MIA!
PIZZA BEER

EVERYONE LOVES PIZZA, AND EVERYONE LOVES BEER, SO it's a wonder this has never been done before. The Mamma Mia! Pizza Beer was created by beer and pizza diehards Tom and Athena Seefurth. The idea was born when the couple (both chefs) found themselves with a surplus of tomatoes. After a bit of research and some conversations with local brewers, Pizza Beer's recipe was developed and the brewing began. To get that moreish pizza flavour, the Seefurths dip an actual margarita pizza into the mash and allow it to steep like a tea bag. The spices wash into the mix, then it's boiled for a long time. Hops and spices are added, the liquid is cooled and then it's all filtered into the final fermentation vessel. Two weeks later, you've got the perfect match for your Friday night gorge-fest.

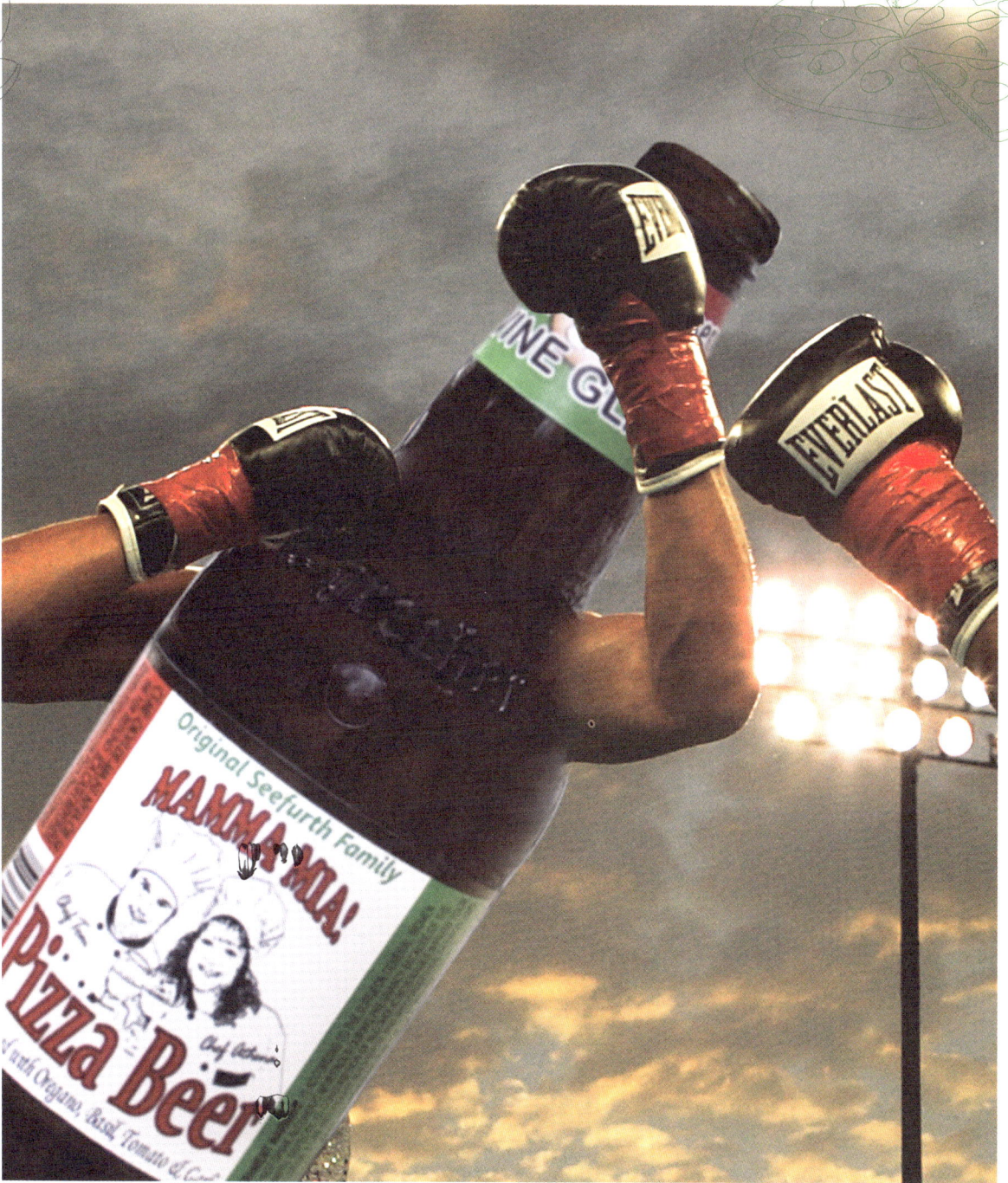

MADE IN
THE UNITED STATES
by

DOCK STREET BREWERY

WALKER

IN A TRIBUTE TO THE POPULAR TELEVISION SERIES *The Walking Dead*, Dock Street Brewery has created 'the smartest beer you'll ever drink'. Walker is an American pale stout brewed with malted wheat, oats, barley and fuggle hops. And what is it that makes it a *Walking Dead* beer? Goats' brains. The brains apparently provide the beer with a subtly smoky flavour, while the addition of cranberries leaves the stout with a reddish (bloody) colour and tartness. Add in a reimaging of Dock Street's sailor logo as a freaky zombie and you've got yourself a fan beer like no other! So much so that the brewery received a phone call from one of the producers of the show wanting to give it a try.

DOCK STREET
BREWING CO.

WALKER
brewed with
roasted goat brains
and cranberries

The Walker of shame.

RED DUCK

LICKY

LIQUORICE IS A DIVISIVE LOLLY. EITHER YOU LOVE IT, OR you want to relegate it to the seventh circle of hell – there are no in-betweens. But Red Duck has good news for those on the 'love' side of the liquorice divide. Licky is a dark lager brewed with dried liquorice root, sarsaparilla root and aniseed myrtle, so if you don't like black jelly beans, it may not be for you. The aroma is distinctly liquorice, but the taste is rather more balanced – no Darrel Lea vibes here. Licky is a lager with a little something different to offer.

LICKY

ALL NATURAL UNFILTERED ALE

RED
DUCK

- LIMITED RELEASE -

LICKY

DARK LICORICE LAGER
5.8% A/V

BEER · PRODUCT OF AUSTRALIA

MADE IN
AUSTRALIA
by

MATSO'S BROOME BREWERY

LYCHEE BEER

LYCHEES ARE A PRETTY WEIRD-LOOKING FRUIT IN THEIR own right. They resemble a long-forgotten dinosaur's egg, or an alien's heart, or the kind of little buzzing creature you'd see in a Jim Henson film. Nonetheless, they are quite delicious, with a soft, fleshy texture (similar to an eyeball, perhaps?). So put some in a beer and add some elderflower and some raw wheat because you're feeling a bit fruity, and you've got yourself a pretty different-tasting blended ale to sip on. Matso's brewed this lychee beer to celebrate Broome's cultural diversity: as they put it, 'If you don't have mixed blood and something weird in the cupboard you're almost not local.'

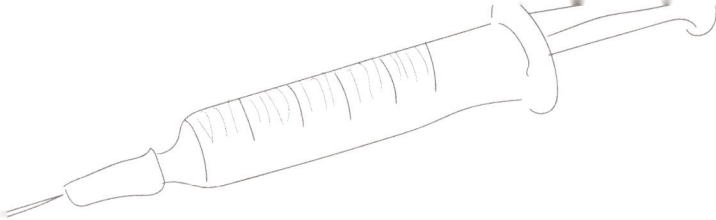

SLINTORY

CLEAR AND RICH TASTE

PRECIOUS フレシャス

コラーゲン2000mg

SPECIAL VALUE AND QUALITY

FOR REFRESHING TIME

MADE IN
JAPAN
by

SUNTORY
PRECIOUS

FANCY A FACE LIFT WITH YOUR BEER? GRAB yourself a Japanese Precious lager and witness those wrinkles melting away. With collagen as an active ingredient in the lager, it's no wonder! While you can't actually taste it, the collagen in the beer is marketed heavily at women, with one of the taglines purportedly quipping, 'Guys can tell if a girl is taking collagen or not.' So watch out, ladies. Chauvinism aside, Precious is an unremarkable light lager that will probably not make you look any younger (sorry).

THE UNITED STATES
by

SHORT'S BREWING COMPANY

BLOODY BEER

THE BELOVED HANGOVER CURE HAS BEEN REIMAGINED FOR those who aren't so keen on vodka before midday but will happily have a beer instead (beer has barley, barley is a cereal, ergo beer = breakfast food). Brewed to replicate a Bloody Mary cocktail, this beer by Short's Brewing is fermented with Roma tomatoes and then spiced with dill, horseradish, peppercorns and celery seed. Following the intense flavour and aroma of tomato juice on the first sip, each of the other spicy flavours makes its way forward so that, like the cocktail, you feel as though you're eating some kind of breakfast with your hair-of-the-dog hangover cure. Drink slightly warm to really taste it all and kick that headache's arse.

Just a few tomatoes ready for the brewing.

MADE IN
THE UNITED STATES
by

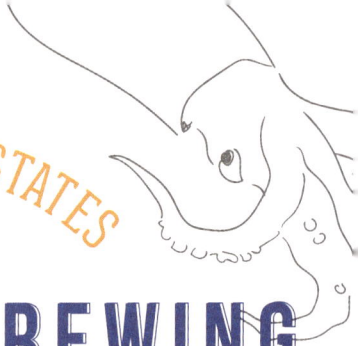

3 SHEEPS BREWING COMPANY

NIMBLE LIPS NOBLE TONGUE VOLUME 3

THE NIMBLE LIPS NOBLE TONGUE SERIES AT 3 SHEEPS Brewing Company gives the brewers a chance to test their creativity. Each volume explores a different style and uses different (and we mean different) ingredients. Volume 3 is an India Pale Ale, but what makes it a little special is the addition of real squid's ink. The reason for this strange ingredient is its colour. Wanting to make a black IPA (yep, a 'pale ale' that's black, go figure), but not wanting to have the heavy flavour of darker roasted malts, the brewers realised that squid's ink could both darken the IPA and enhance its hoppiness. It also left the beer with a slight briny flavour. So no gimmicks here, folks, all business from 3 Sheeps.

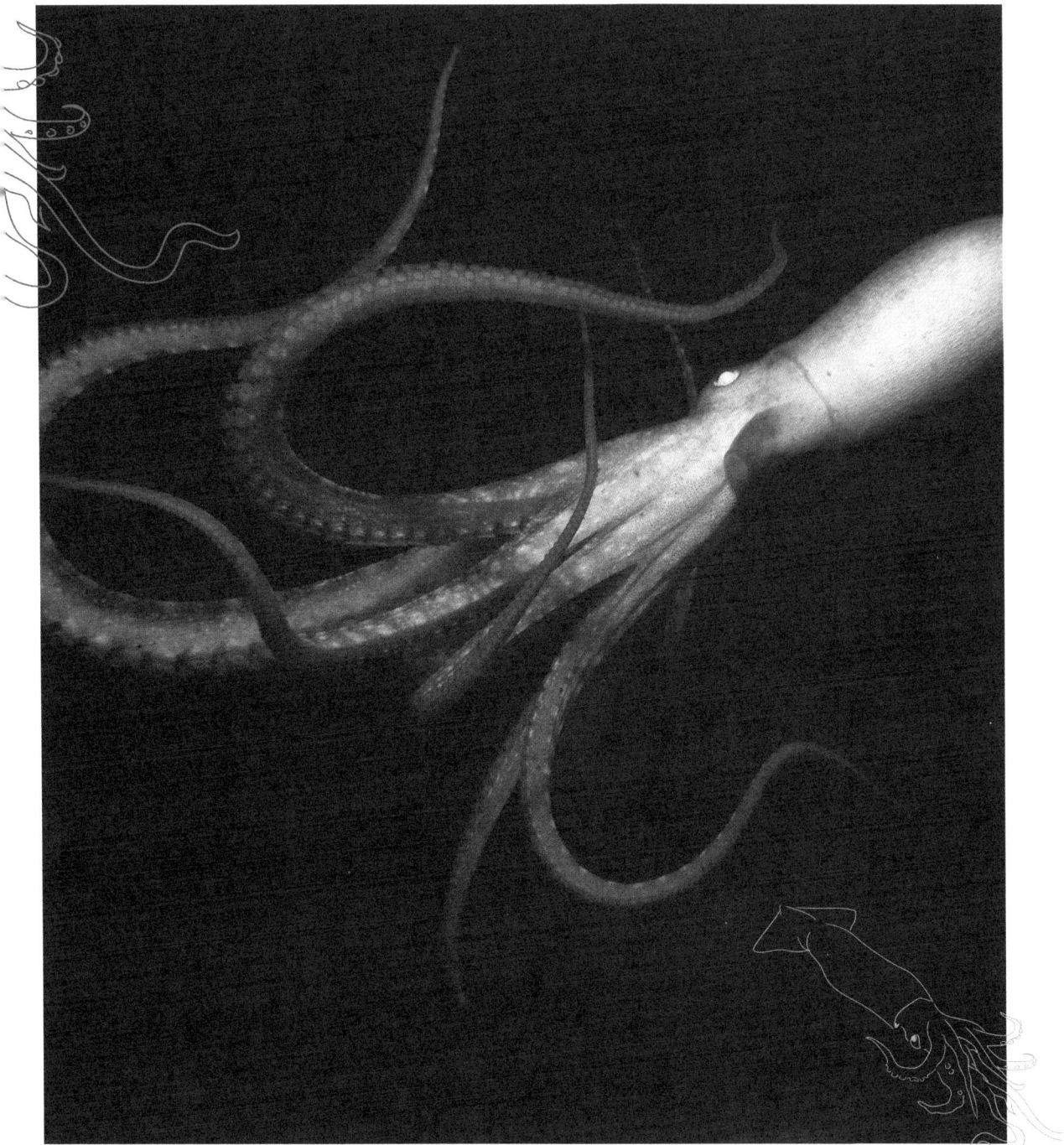

ROGUE ALES

VOODOO DOUGHNUT BACON MAPLE ALE

BACON. MAPLE. WHAT MORE DO WE NEED TO SAY ABOUT this out-there brew? It's a brown ale, if you must know. It's really sweet, as you would expect, and at the same time kind of smoky and spicy because of the bacon. But most importantly, you need it in your life. Don't muck around here, people, this is a beer with bacon, maple and doughnuts. What are you waiting for? You'll never have to order dessert again.

Rogue's brewmaster John Maier at Rogue Farms, where they grow ingredients for their beers, spirits, ciders and sodas.

THE UNITED STATES
by

FOSSIL FUELS BREWING COMPANY

ANCIENT WHEAT

SEEKING TO CREATE A NEW TYPE OF ANTIBIOTIC, MEDICAL mycologist Raul Cano extracted bacteria from the gut of an amber-encased bee – a bee anywhere between 25 million and 45 million years old. (*Jurassic Park*, eat your heart out!) But just when you thought Sam Neil was about to crash through the door and start smashing up test tubes, the antibiotics didn't work. Cano, being a glass-half-full kinda guy, thought the next best thing would be to brew a beer from it – obviously. The bee's guts were used as the yeast strain in an 'ancient' German-style wheat beer with a clean, citrusy zing. And just a hint of rampaging T-Rex.

FOSSIL FUELS
BREWING

trade (45) *mark*

Ancient Beer

by

WILLIAMS BROS. BREWING COMPANY

KELPIE

DESPITE BEING SLIMY, UGLY AND CONSTANTLY TANGLING around your legs when you just want to swim, seaweed is quite useful. For one, it's an excellent fertiliser. The Scottish have been chucking piles of kelp on their garden beds for hundreds of years, and coastal breweries would even fertilise their fields of barley with the stuff, giving the final beer a very particular, seaweedy taste. The inclusion of actual seaweed in William Bros' Kelpie is all about recreating this oceanic flavour and aroma, catching a bit of that taste of the good old days (or not-so-good old days, depending on your feelings about Viking raids). Kelpie is a dark ale with a chocolatey, salty and malty taste that's so delicious it might just change how you feel about seaweed.

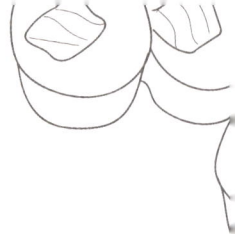

RED DUCK

FORSAKEN

FORSAKEN IS A WEIRD BEER IN DISGUISE: IN A BLIND tasting you wouldn't think there was any more to it than to any other tasty dark-red ale. But like so many of Red Duck's brews, this beer is very far from average. Made with black, white and red rice as well as the more standard barley and oats, plus roasted wattleseeds and nori seaweed, this beer is possibly the closest thing you could ever get to a liquid nori roll. Considering the rice content and the fact Forsaken was fermented with a famous strain of sake yeast, it could be argued that this is really a sake sneakily disguised as a red ale, or that it's a hybrid of some kind (Red Duck call it a 'Japanese Red Sake Ale', which could just catch on). Or, you could just accept that it's yet another example of how broad the definition of 'beer' really is.

Red Duck brewery.

by

THE LOST ABBEY

GIFT OF MAGI

WHETHER THEY'RE 'KINGS', 'WISE MEN' OR 'MAGI', THE story of the three strange men turning up at baby Jesus' manger in Bethlehem is a familiar one. Each brought a rare and expensive gift – though they weren't exactly newborn-friendly (babies don't tend to be all that into perfume and ointments, but hey, a gift's a gift). They'd probably have been better off just bringing along a few brewskis to split with the shepherds and get the party rolling, and if Lost Abbey had been around, they would have had the perfect beer for the occasion. No doubt, the Gift of Magi golden ale is fit for the son of God. Brewed with the bark of frankincense, gold in colour (bit of a cheat there) and with a dash of myrrh, it incorporates the main points of the story to create a truly divine seasonal Christmas ale.

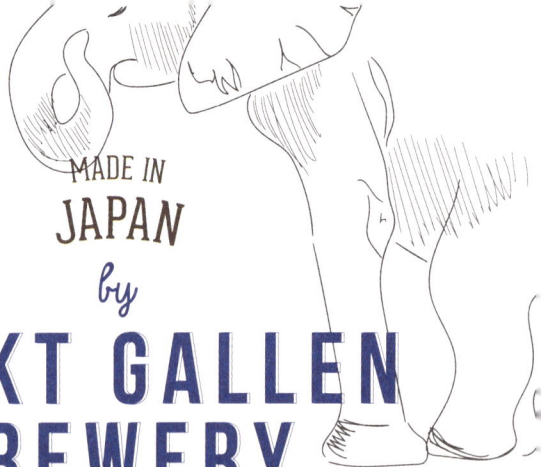

by

SANKT GALLEN BREWERY

UN, KONO KURO

ELEPHANTS ARE BEAUTIFUL CREATURES. INTELLIGENT, DEEP and emotional, they remind us of the best parts of humanity – without all the bombs and motivational speakers. We love them. But how far does that love stretch? Ask yourself, would you eat elephant poo? It's definitely not the worst poo you could eat, but it tends to come in pretty huge servings. That poo has a lot in common with the Un, Kono Kuro coffee stout – definitely not the worst beer to drink, and pretty big ... and no, this isn't just a really questionable segue, because this beer also involves actual elephant poo. The connection here is the coffee beans used in the brewing process. As with 'kopi lewak', the world-famous civet-poo coffee, the beans used in this beer were digested by an elephant first. The coffee is called 'black ivory', and it's as rare as it is ~~overpriced~~ intriguing – again, just like this beer, which sold out within minutes of release. That doesn't mean you can't still eat elephant poo, though.

Sankt()allen

うん、
この
黒

Cannabia

Smelli, Smell & Smile™

www.cannabia.com

First hemp beverage of mankind. The original. Primer bebita con cáñamo.

Cannabia

Das Hanfgetränk

e 0,33l   ORGANIC*

Since 1996

BIO

Das erste hanfhaltige Getränk der Welt. Das Original.

HANFGETRÄNK · BIERE AU CHANVRE · CERVE...
HEMP BEER · BIER & HENNEP MIX · ...
DE CANHAMO · BEVANDA A BASE DI BIRRA E ...
ΗΔΙΔΚΤΟ ΠΟΤΟ ΜΠΥΡΑΣ ΜΕ ΚΑΝΝΑΒΗ

DUPETIT

CANNABIA

DON'T GET TOO EXCITED – ALTHOUGH THIS BEER IS BREWED with hemp, it won't get you high. Hemp actually has many of the characteristics that brewers use hops for, including taste and smell. In this cheeky beer, hemp flowers are used as well as hop flowers to create a floral, spicy, even citrusy flavour and aroma. Dupetit, who also produces hemp perfumes, cosmetics and 'sweets', proudly reports that it is the 'first legal hemp drink of mankind since 1996', which is really quite an achievement for the species. It's dry at the finish, like your mouth after smoking a joint (... at least, that's what we've heard), but no need to stock up on chips, as there are no reports that Cannabia gives you the munchies.

8 WIRED BREWING COMPANY

BUMAYE

NEW ZEALAND'S 8 WIRED BREWERY HAS CREATED A BIG, strong, aggressive fighter here – but not without sophistication. Taken from Congolese, *bumaye* literally translates to 'kill him', and became a catch-phrase after Muhammad Ali's renowned 'Rumble in the Jungle' with George Foreman in Zaire (now the Democratic Republic of Congo). The locals took a shine to Ali, chanting, '*Ali, bumaye!*' throughout the fight. At 16 per cent, this imperial stout is sure to punch you in the teeth, but being aged in pinot noir barrels for 16 months has left an impression on this misunderstood giant, mellowing it and encouraging it to mature and leave its fighting days behind. 8 Wired has said Bumaye is the most aggressive beer they have made to date, but it's a delicious one nonetheless.

MADE IN
THE UNITED STATES
by

JESTER KING BREWERY

GOTLANDSDRICKA

WITH A NAME MEANING 'DRINK OF THE LAND OF THE Goths', this is the kind of beer that carries an axe and wears a helmet with two horns attached. Touted as the beer of Vikings, Jester King's creation is based on the farmhouse ales brewed on the island of Gotland, near Sweden. The malt is smoked with birchwood and then brewed with juniper, rye and sweet gale. In reality, it's probably quite a different beverage to the one those Vikings would have swilled before heading out for a spot of raping and pillaging, but given their penchant for sacrificing horses after a drink or two, that's probably not a bad thing.

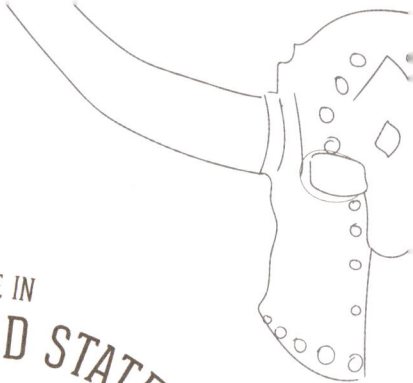

CHARLES WELLS BREWING

YOUNG'S DOUBLE CHOCOLATE STOUT

WHAT'S BETTER THAN SINGLE CHOCOLATE? WE THINK YOU know the answer. Why drink a single chocolate stout when you could have a double chocolate stout? Young's Double Chocolate Stout is packed full of real dark chocolate and chocolate essence to create a decadent and rich flavour that's, surprisingly, not too sweet. And if the ad campaign that went with this delightful drink is anything to go by, this stout's flavour could be likened to a muscular fellow lifting two adorable kittens. We're not totally sure what that entails, but hey, it's double chocolate! So just drink it.

SERIOUS STOUT

...with just a bit of sweet.

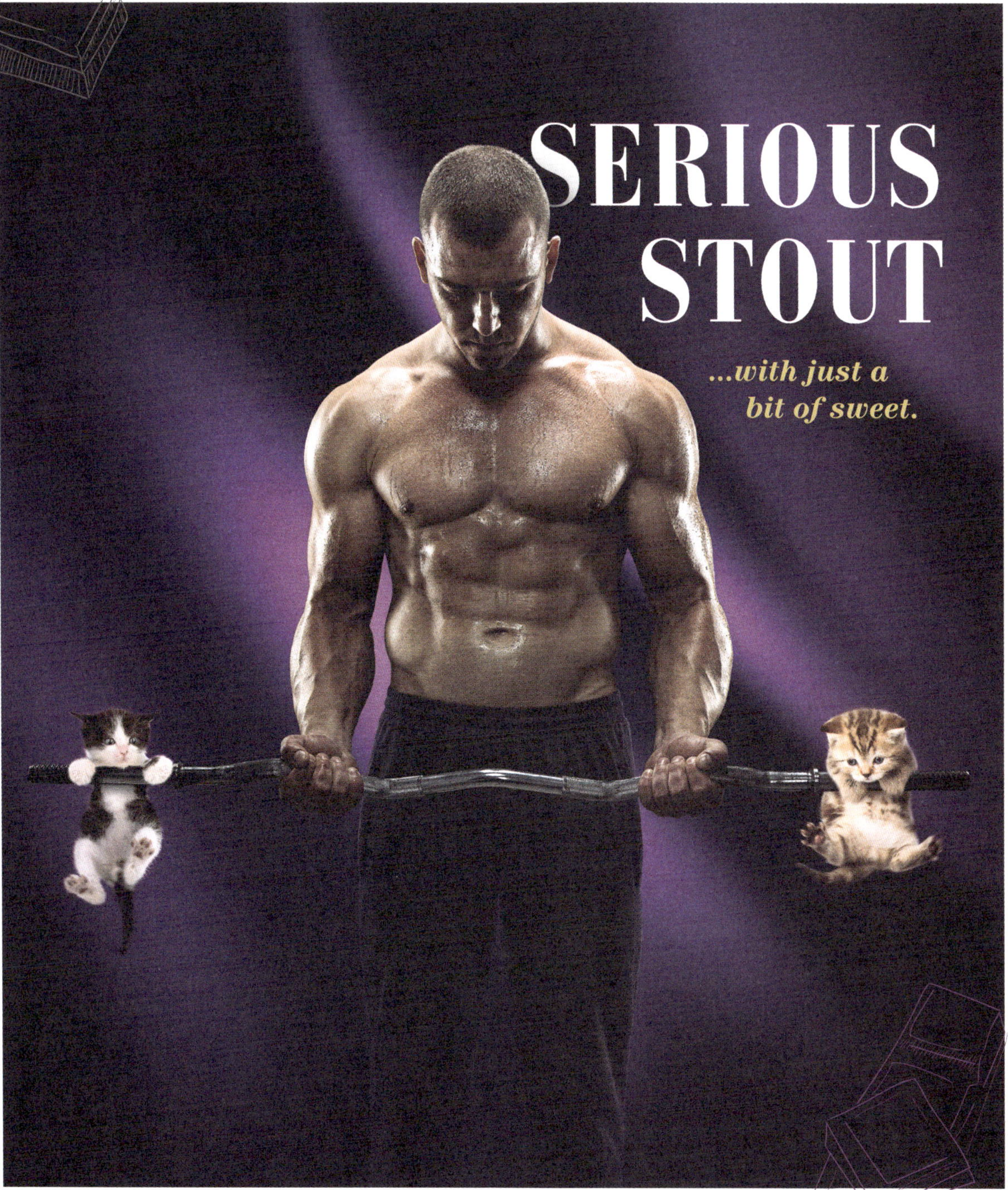

BELVOIR BREWERY

THE BLUE BREW

IT'S A SURPRISE THAT THIS LITTLE ENGLISH LORD DOESN'T smell like a gymnast's shoe. Oh, yes, we see the rising panic in your face, but rest assured, there are no socks in this brew. Only stilton whey. What's stilton whey, you ask? We had to google it too, but it turns out that it's the cloudy, watery by-product of the Brits' beloved stilton blue cheese. Indeed, this appealing substance is added to the beer wort, and then all those cheesy, beery flavours are left to ferment together. It's a creamy drop with a touch of saltiness, although sadly it's not speckled with blue. Enjoy with a cracker and some quince paste.

·BELVOIR·

BLUE BREW

"The King of British Ales"

Stilton Infused Beer

4.2%

Alc. Vol

JESTER KING BREWERY

AMICIS MORTIS

FEELING A BIT MORBID? WELL, THERE'S A BEER FOR THAT.
Jester King has done it again with Amicis Mortis, a beer containing sweet potato, coconut and chilli. This unusual farmhouse ale was actually inspired by a spicy sweet potato and coconut meal that the creators enjoyed one night. This sort of explains things, but it really does make you worry at how impressionable brewers are. The 'death' part is a bit more symbolic: according to Jester King, the word 'coconut' comes from old Spanish for 'skull', the chilli is part of the 'nightshade' family, known for its use in poisons, and sweet potato is part of the 'morning glory' family, which often symbolises mortality. Cheery. Still, Amicis Mortis is an easygoing brew that's worth a try, if only so you can brag to everyone that you've tasted death and lived to tell the tale.

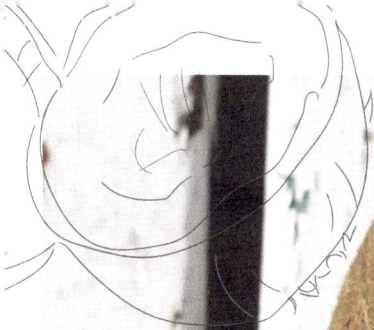

RED DUCK

CACTUS

HAVE YOU EVER SEEN A PRICKLY PEAR CACTUS? JUST IN case you haven't, picture a cactus with heaps of other little cacti growing off it to create one giant mutant cactus – not unlike a Megatron–cactus hybrid. If that didn't make any sense, don't worry about it. This beer was brewed in collaboration with Brian Strumke from Stillwater Artisanal. It's a farmhouse ale, barrel-aged for nine months in French oak. And the cactus connection? There's prickly pear in the brew, along with some agave syrup (agave being the plant used to make tequila). The result is a brew that's funkier than John Travolta on a Saturday night. It's also a standout beer on the courage front, as the prickly pears all had to be hand-picked by someone willing to brave more than their fair share of spikes and scratches. All in the name of beer.

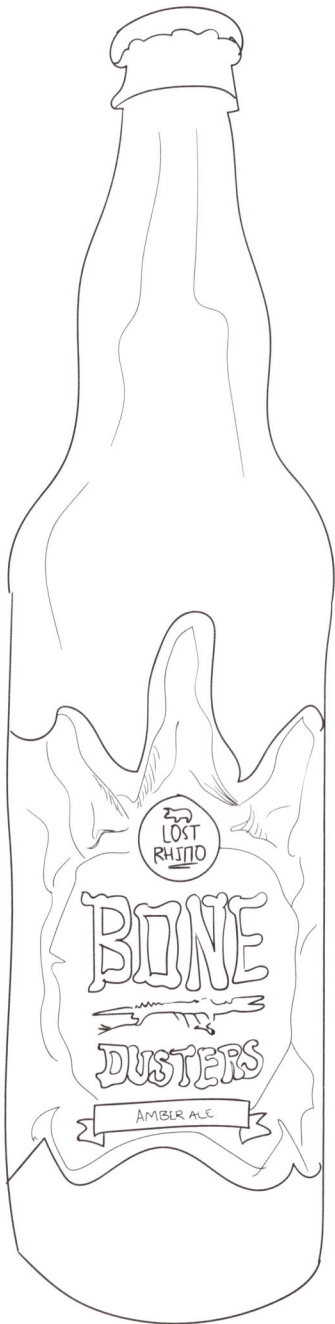

MADE IN
THE UNITED STATES
by

LOST RHINO BREWING COMPANY

BONE DUSTERS AMBER ALE

JASON OSBORNE IS THE CO-FOUNDER OF PALEO QUEST, A non-profit organisation dedicated to advancing palaeontology and geology. He likes diving for fossils in swamps and rivers that contain sharks, alligators, heavy currents, little visibility and heaps of trees. But don't we all? On one such dive, he found the fossil of a 35 million-year-old whalebone and thought, *Why not swab this old whale bone for yeast to make beer?* Osborne enlisted the help of Lost Rhino Brewing Company's Jasper Akerboom, and together they found a whole new strain of brewing yeast – *Saccharomyces cerevisiae var protocetus*, named after the protocetid whale fossil it was swabbed from. Wild yeast strains like this one create wacky flavours, and in Bone Dusters' case, the resulting brew is Belgian in style with heavy citrus characteristics.

Jason Osborne [left] and Jasper Akerboom [right] swabbing for yeast samples on prehistoric whale bones at the Calvert Marine Museum. Solomon's Island. Maryland.

NEW BELGIUM BREWING COMPANY

COCONUT CURRY HEFEWEIZEN

DINNER AND BEER ALL IN ONE! THIS HEFEWEIZEN BY NEW Belgium in the States is packed full of curry-worthy flavours, such as cinnamon, coriander, fenugreek, ginger, kaffir lime and cayenne pepper. It has coconut added for good measure, and you get a hint of banana coming through, which is a common flavour in hefes added by the distinctive yeast strains used in their brewing. Overall, it's big and bold and full of flavour, spicy but also kind of sweet. Drink with some naan bread for an authentic experience.

New Belgium's quality assurance lab, hard at work.

ROGUE ALES

CHIPOTLE ALE

THIS AMBER ALE FROM ROGUE COMES WITH A WORD OF warning. Jalapenos are spicy little devils, and this beer comes packed full of them. They've been smoked for extra flavour, leaving the final product tasting malty, smoky and spicy – chipotles are smoked and dried jalapenos, FYI. The chipotle spice hits you at the back of the throat, but it's not quite as intense as biting down on a real one (so rest assured, your head will remain attached to your body). If you're the type of person who always avoids that extra hot chipotle sauce, then this may not be the ale for you. But if you love watering eyes and a runny nose, then pour yourself a glass – maybe just make sure you've got a glass of milk close by.

Rogue's brewmaster John Maier.

MADE IN
THE UNITED STATES
by

FLYING DOG BREWERY

PEARL NECKLACE CHESAPEAKE STOUT

HERE'S A BEER TO DRINK WITH A LOVER. AND NO, WE'RE not talking about that kind of pearl necklace, so get your minds out of the gutters. Despite looking like little bits of phlegm, oysters are, they say, an aphrodisiac. So in the name of romance and romantics everywhere, Flying Dog have gone right ahead and added oysters to the brew of their Chesapeake stout. Proceeds from the beer even go towards oyster restoration efforts in Chesapeake Bay. So, while you're drinking this beer and getting a little bit frisky, you can feel good about saving the oysters so that future generations can get a bit frisky too.

MADE IN
THE UNITED STATES
by

BALLAST POINT BREWING COMPANY

PEPPERMINT VICTORY AT SEA

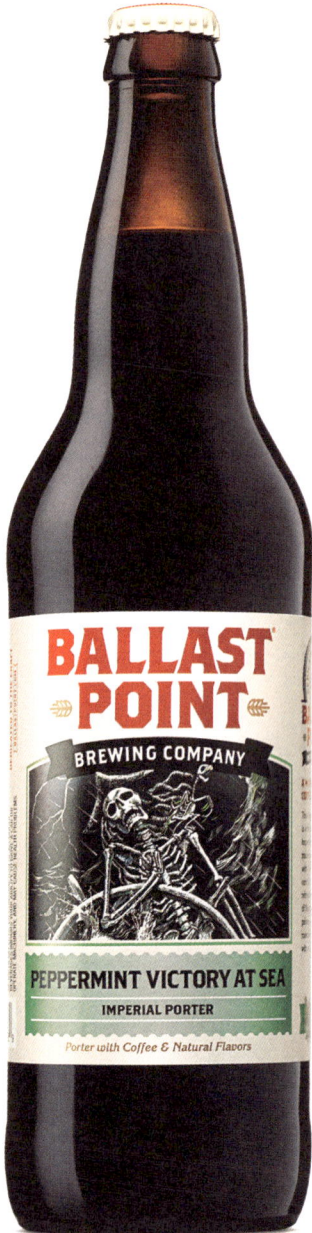

BACK IN THE DARK DAYS, WHEN YOU WERE A SELF-CONSCIOUS teenager, ordering coffee to impress the other self-conscious teenagers, did you always order a flavoured latte? Oh, no, neither did we ... but, you know, do you remember when that was a thing in the mid-2000s? Well, Peppermint Victory at Sea takes that fairly lame trend and turns it into something rather magical – an imperial porter infused with coffee beans, vanilla *and* peppermint. We're talking a serious attack of malt and hops, smoothed out with all the sweet comfort of a cosy, if stained, corner couch at Gloria Jean's. So the next time you're at a bar and want to impress the other self-conscious adults by ordering a dark beer, coffee with vanilla and peppermint saves the day again! Fresh to death.

A Ballast Point brewer pouring a brew.

INDEPENDENCE BREWING COMPANY

CONVICT HILL STOUT

OATMEAL, THE WARM AND NUTRITIOUS BREAKFAST OPTION otherwise known as 'porridge' (a word as ugly as a word can be), probably doesn't leap out as a great flavour for a beer. But it's actually a fairly popular style of stout, known generally and sensibly as 'oatmeal stout' (cos let's face it, nobody's buying 'porridge stout'). The use of oats in the beer mash creates a sweet flavour and an out-of-this-world smoothness. To take that to the next level, Convict Hill Stout is brewed with chocolate malt on top of the standard roasted barley and oat flakes. It's not lumpy and sludgy like oatmeal is when it gets cold, though; it's a thick, creamy brew that's a little bit bitter and a lot better than actual oatmeal.

Independence Brewing Company's brewer Brannon Radicke doing his thing.

ODELL BREWING COMPANY

LUGENE CHOCOLATE MILK STOUT

IN FORT COLLINS, COLORADO, WHERE ODELL BREWING Company is based, there is a farmer called Lugene. For over a decade, Lugene has been hauling the spent grains from Odell's brews to feed to his dairy cows. In a true 'circle of life' moment (*The Lion King* soundtrack plays), milk from the cows that have been eating the grains is used to brew the Lugene Chocolate Milk Stout. Milk stouts have a long history – in the 1800s, they were served to British labourers as a 'restorative' and 'strengthening' beverage – and eventually brewers figured out how to extract the lactose (also known as 'milk sugar') to be used in the brewing process. So, no, they don't just pour the milk straight in. In Odell's case, the milk sugar from Lugene's malty cow juice is added to the brew along with some milk chocolate, and so a king is born.

BANANA INVESTMENTS LIMITED

RAHA

LET'S TAKE A TRIP AWAY FROM EXPERIMENTAL CRAFT brewers to a beer that's actually a bit of a staple in many East African countries. RAHA is a banana beer, brewed purely by fermenting mashed bananas. There's no hops, no barley, none of the usuals in this one – just the ever-surprising banana and some maize, the source of wild yeast that will get the fermentation going. It has a sweet taste and packs a punch at 11 per cent alcohol content. But bananas aren't as simple as you might think. Two types are used in the brew: igikashi, which has a full-on taste, and the milder igisahira. The mash used in the beer consists of one third igikashi and two thirds igisahira – so bananas and maths combine to offer you a very different style of beer in RAHA.

MADE IN
THE UNITED STATES
by

ROGUE ALES

SRIRACHA HOT STOUT

WE'VE SHOWN YOU A BLOW-YOUR-HEAD-OFF CHILLI WHEAT beer, but what about a blow-your-face-off hot sauce stout? Sriracha HOT Stout from Rogue is brewed with the much-loved Huy Fong hot chilli sauce, so it's bloody hot and bloody dark. Likely to remind you of that time you accidently squeezed the hot sauce bottle too hard and covered your Vietnamese noodles in red, this stout will not apologise to your mouth after you swallow it. Rogue suggests matching this beer with anything that you want to finish off with a spicy kick – whether that be a hamburger, a nice pasta, a relationship, your job …

ROGUE

SRIRACHA **HOT** STOUT BEER

ROGUE ROOSTER SAUCE

男敢 冒险 图益

ROGUE ALES & SPIRITS
2320 OSU Drive, Newport, OR 97365
(541) 867-3660 www.rogue.com

1 PT. 9.4 FL. OZ. / 750 ML

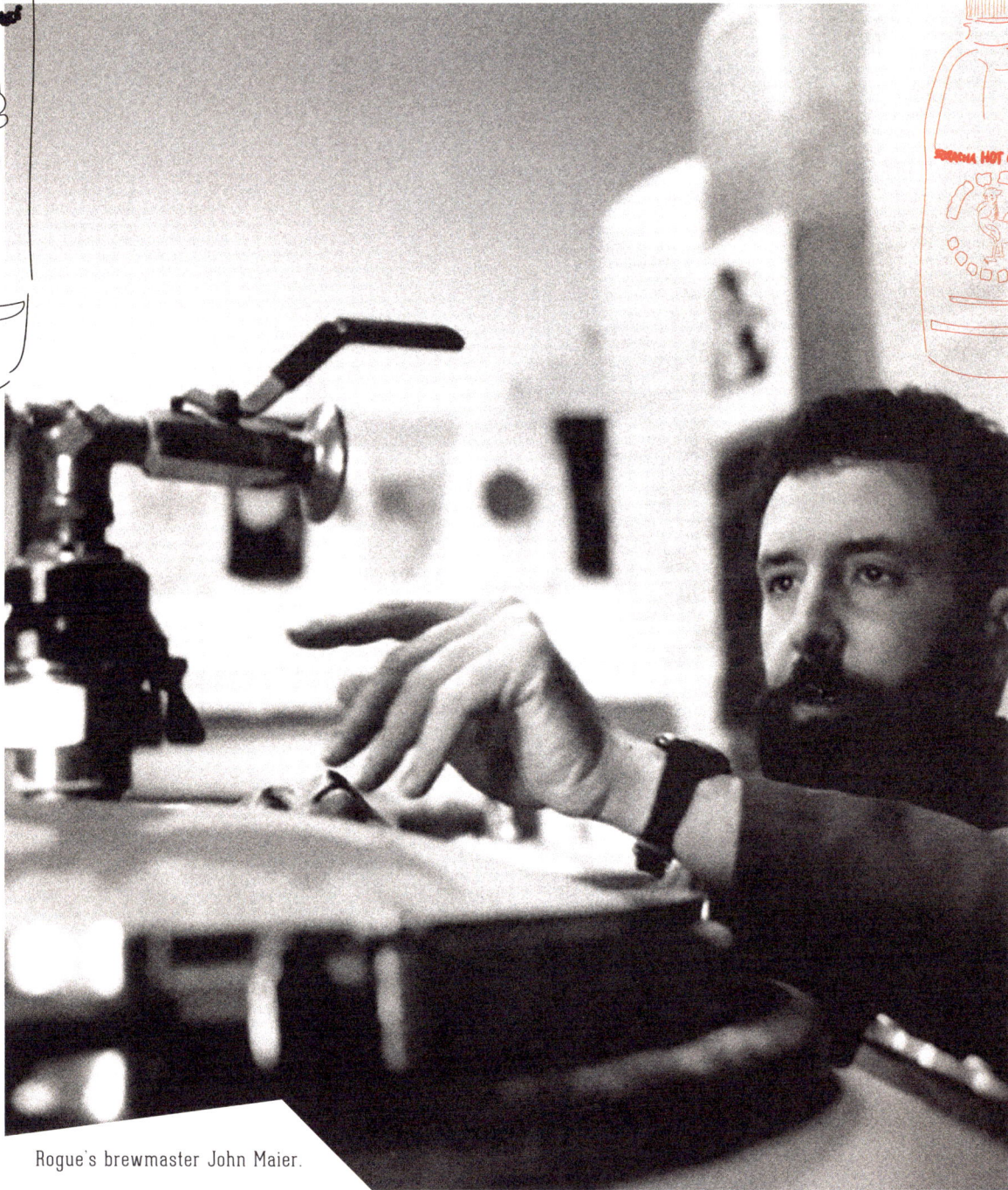

Rogue's brewmaster John Maier.

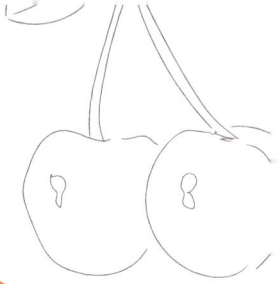

MADE IN

THE UNITED STATES

by

RIGHT BRAIN BREWERY

CHERRY PIE WHOLE

CHERRY PIE IS REALLY DELICIOUS. BEER IS THE BEST DRINK. Eighty cherry pies are better than one. These are all established and universally accepted facts. But Right Brain Brewery has shown some serious nous and added them together to create Cherry Pie Whole. It's an amber ale made with eighty whole cherry pies – we're talking crust and all thrown straight into the vat. It tastes like cherries (obviously) but also has notes of bubble gum and buttered toast. How could you not drink this beer all the time?

Right Brain's Jeff Houser adding 18 kilos of Michigan cherries into the boil kettle to make Cherry Pie Whole.

by

BROUWERIJ BOSTEELS

DEUS

THIS IS THE PERFECT BEER FOR A CELEBRATION. COMPLETE with a cork ready to pop out and hit the ceiling (or someone's eye), DeuS is really a hybrid between beer and champagne. It looks like champagne, it sounds like champagne, it's fermented like champagne (in inverted bottles), but it's still a beer brewed entirely from barley. It could be the swankiest beer of them all. You can even get your wine snob on, take a good sniff and proclaim that you can smell apples, mint, ginger, thyme, citrus, pears and cloves. It's the perfect beer to get fancy with.

BEYOND THE BEST OF

DEUS

Brut des Flandres

Cuvée Prestige 2002

JESTER KING BREWERY

HIBERNAL DICHOTOMOUS

ANOTHER ONE FROM THESE CRAZY GENIUSES – BUT CAN YOU guess what's in the farmhouse ale this time? It's easy, all you have to do is think of three totally unconnected ingredients! Placed your bets? Right, the 2015 Hibernal Dichotomous is brewed with beets, oranges and thyme. It's one of a series of beers based on seasons: this one is all about winter, boarding yourself up in a cave (i.e. your blanket fort), living off root vegetables and getting enough vitamin C to tide you over the season of sickness. The beets are shredded, the oranges are squeezed and peeled, and the thyme is just chucked in there before the whole lot is fermented for a good six weeks. And it actually works. The flavours unite to make a pink-tinged wintry beer that goes perfectly with a pair of warm trackies and a rainy weekend of Netflix.

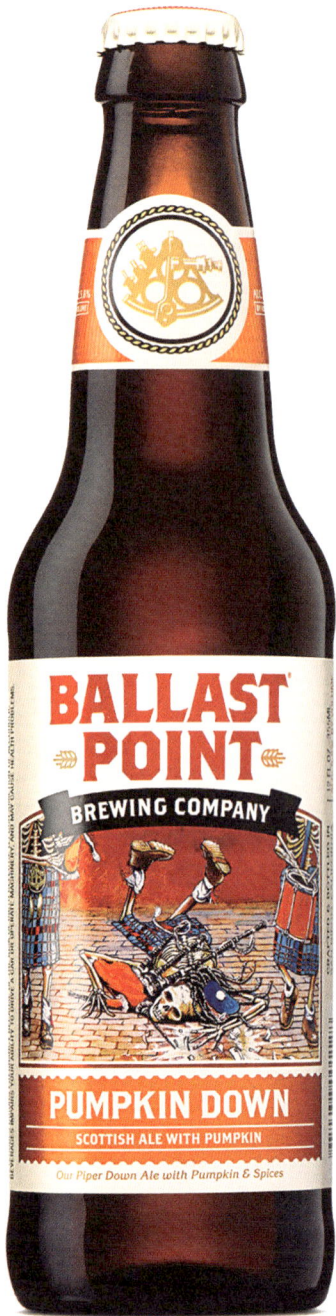

MADE IN THE UNITED STATES by

BALLAST POINT BREWING COMPANY

PUMPKIN DOWN

BUTTERBEER, ANYONE? SURELY BALLAST POINT'S PUMPKIN Down is the drink our mate J.K. had in mind when she sent her intrepid witches and wizards off for a drink at the local. Its base is Ballast Point's Piper Down Scottish ale, which is full of caramel and toffee maltiness that sounds bloody good in its own right. But then they add a bucket-load of roasted pumpkin and some complementary spices, and the end product could almost certainly be served in the Hog's Head. (If you don't know what we're talking about here, then you had a very sad childhood and we are sorry.) This ale is even more proof that vegetables are not evil and should be consumed, even if only in beers.

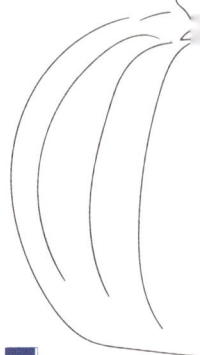

THE UNITED STATES
by

JACK'S ABBY CRAFT LAGERS

FIRE IN THE HAM

AHH, CAMPING. STORIES AROUND THE FIRE, MARSHMALLOWS and stargazing ... and waking up to find that every centimetre of your clothes, hair and skin reeks of smoke. Hell, your kidneys probably even smell like smoke. Don't you just love camping? (This is a question that has sparked many a family feud.) This beer is basically that experience in a glass (the campfire smokiness, we mean, not the feuds). Most of the malts for this lager are dried over flaming beechwood and the final product smells of smoked ham and bacon – which is rather mysterious, considering it's actually vegan friendly, with not a smidge of piggie in the brew. Drink one while sitting by the campfire for that really smoky experience.

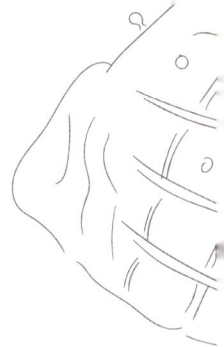

HELLO KITTY BEER

IN ASIA THERE IS A HELLO KITTY BRANDED VERSION OF just about every product imaginable. So why should beer miss out on having a slightly creepy, mouthless cat mascot to help move it off the shelves? Available in peach, lemon-lime, passionfruit and banana flavours, these fruity beverages are really low in alcohol (around 2.3 per cent) and really high in sugar. Sounds like a drink a kid would enjoy, right? By all accounts, the drink tastes more like sweet fruit juice than a regular beer, and the cans are all colourful and fun and strangely similar to products marketed at children ... Not that we're insinuating anything, of course – after all, cute anthropomorphised cartoon animals are totally a grown-up thing too. Cough.

TWO BIRDS BREWING

TACO

WHEN TWO BIRDS FOUNDERS JAYNE AND DANIELLE TOOK A trip to California, they found what many people who travel to California seem to find ... no, not shattered dreams and failed marriages: *inspiration*. The brewers decided to create a beer inspired by their favourite not-actually-Californian-but-close-enough food: tacos. Yes indeed, the most beloved and easily transportable of Mexican food items has been translated into liquid form, though you won't find any shredded meat or bits of tortilla floating in there (luckily). Taco is brewed with its namesake's staple flavours: corn, coriander leaf and fresh lime (peel), creating fresh, zesty flavours that are perfect to wash down a Mexican feast. Delicioso!

Random guy eating a taco.

MADE IN

THE UNITED STATES

by

ANDERSON VALLEY BREWING COMPANY

BRINEY MELON GOSE

LOOK CLOSELY AT THIS LABEL AND YOU MAY HAVE SOME questions: what is 'gose'? Why is it 'briney'? Is that bear wearing antlers as a costume or is it some bear-deer hybrid? We can't answer all of those questions, but we can guess that you were so distracted by them that you didn't notice the big watermelon in the sky. (Or maybe you did, in which case reward yourself with a beer.) Anderson Valley's Briney Melon Gose is a watermelon ale that's as thirst-quenching as a sparkling stream but a little more tart. A gose is a top-fermented beer with a characteristic whack of saltiness, and that added pinch of sea salt balances what could have been a fruity sweetness overload. The result is pure summer: like eating watermelon after a dip in the ocean.

THE UNITED STATES
by
GREAT LAKES BREWING COMPANY

THE OLDEST BEER RECIPE

HISTORY AND BEER UNITE AGAIN, IN THE GREAT LAKES Brewing Company's 5000-year-old beer recipe. The brewing process was taken from an ancient hymn to Ninkasi, the Sumerian (modern-day Southern Iraq) goddess of beer, and was developed with help from archaeologists from the University of Chicago. To be as authentic as possible, they used clay pots and a wooden spoon, and even made an ancient 'beer bread' called 'bappir' as a yeast source (the brewers reckon airborne yeast was the main player, but the bread did play a part). Great Lakes tells us that the end result is very different to modern-day beer, tasting very sour and, at times, acetic, but it's drinkable and has been enjoyed by the brewers and their guests. All hail Ninkasi.

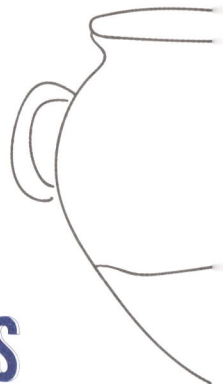

MADE IN

THE UNITED STATES

by

RIGHT BRAIN BREWERY

SPEAR BEER

WHAT COULD BE IN THIS BEER FOR ITS NAME TO BE 'SPEAR'
Beer? Ancient spearheads? The hair shaved from Britney's scalp? Sadly, neither of those are correct, but the real answer is still a bit out there: it's only the ultimate spear of the vegetable family – asparagus. And if you're thinking, *I don't even like asparagus on a plate, as if I'd drink it*, then you'd best skip to the next page. But if you're thinking, *Asparagus is the food of the gods and the greatest of nature's gifts*, then you're in for a treat. This beer smells like asparagus and it tastes like asparagus and if you say asparagus often enough it starts sounding really odd. Asparagus. Lemon peel has also been added to the brew, because why not? It all comes together into a light and summery beer that may or may not make your urine smell strange.

MADE IN
AUSTRALIA
by

MOON DOG CRAFT BREWERY

JUMPING THE SHARK

ANY TELEVISION DIE-HARD WORTH THEIR SALT WOULD recognise 'jumping the shark' as the signal of a show on the wane – a moment when producers stretch plausibility beyond the limit. Each year, Moon Dog try to outdo themselves with the most outrageous beer they can imagine. Take, for instance, 2013's Jumping the Shark, a 15.4 per cent imperial stout that was aged in cognac barrels and infused with 4.5 kilos of Tasmanian black truffles ($4000-worth of Tasmanian black truffles, that is). Co-owner Josh Uljans proudly states that it was probably the most delicious beer Moon Dog's ever made. Although this brew changes every year, it's always monstrous, with a very high alcohol content and all the flavours you're least expecting. 2015's Jumping the Shark was an 18.4 per cent freeze-distilled imperial rye stout aged in rye whisky barrels – just so you know.

Moon Dog brewery.

MERCHANT BREWING COMPANY

EARL PEAR

FANCY A CUPPA? MERCHANT BREWING COMPANY HAS created a beer you can drink cold with lemon – like an iced tea, only better because it's beer. It's a blonde ale with bonus sophistication, and the addition of earl grey tea is sure to get it invited to all the fancy soirées. Plus, just because it's a great idea, they've gone and added pear to the mix too, creating a sweet, fruity and floral beer that'll have you with your pinky in the air like nobody's business. This fine beverage is perfect to serve to your nanna on the verandah (add in some scones and a few sneaky top-ups to get her telling all sort of stories you don't want to hear).

EARL PEAR

EARL GREY TEA AND PEAR

BLONDE ALE

6.4% ABV

330ml

EPIC BREWING COMPANY

COFFEE & FIG EPICUREAN

EPIC BREWING COMPANY'S EPICUREAN SERIES IS DESIGNED to celebrate flavours and aromas that brewers and chefs alike use in their creations. This tasty treat is an imperial oatmeal stout with the addition of caramelised dried figs, whole coffee beans and toasted coconut. Thank god for creative brewing! Figs are underrated at the best of times, so to have *caramelised* figs, no less, in a delicious creamy stout is enough to set a mad world to rights. Epic Brewing suggests drinking a glass with a scoop of vanilla ice-cream, and, um, yes. Just yes.

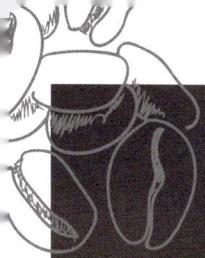

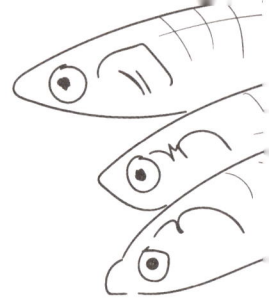

WHEATY BREWING CORPS

ALICI NERO

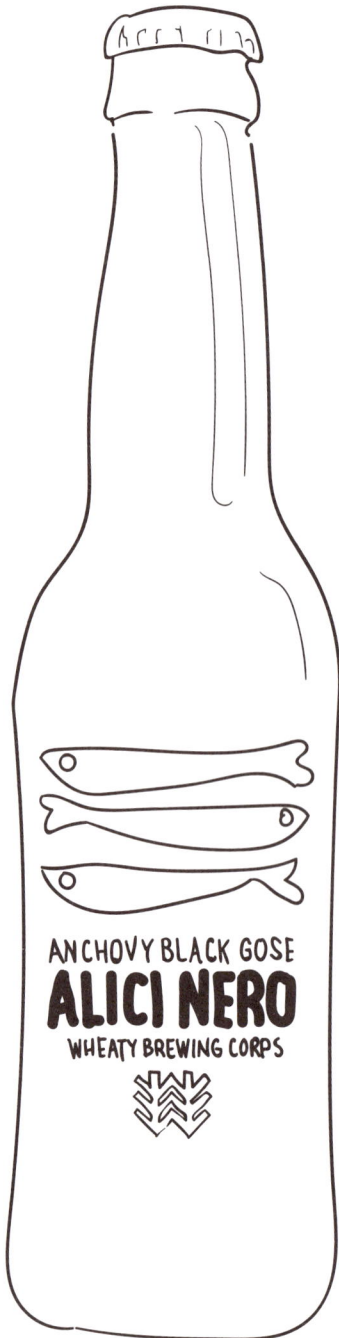

ANCHOVIES - THOSE TINY HAIRY LITTLE FISH THAT YOU either love or hate. Whether it be on a pizza or in your Caesar salad's dressing, you'll taste the salty lifeblood of an anchovy the second it enters your mouth, and for those who hate the things, they have an infuriating tendency to pop up in a meal whenever they're least expected. So how about in a beer? Wheaty Brewing Corps's Alici Nero is a gose, which is already a salty, sour style of beer. So ramping it up with a few white anchovy fillets really gets that little spurting spit thing happening. This is a very savoury beer for those who like some serious salt (and aren't grossed out by tiny hairy fish).

ANCHOVY BLACK GOSE
ALICI NERO
WHEATY BREWING CORPS

THE MASTERMINDS

3 SHEEPS BREWING COMPANY

1327 Huron Ave.
Sheboygan, WI 53081, United States
3sheepsbrewing.com

4 PINES BREWING COMPANY

Manly Brewpub
29/43-45 East Esplanade
Manly NSW 2095, Australia
4pinesbeer.com.au

8 WIRED BREWING COMPANY

26 Glenmore Dr,
Warkworth 0910, New Zealand
8wired.co.nz

ANDERSON VALLEY BREWING COMPANY

17700 Highway 253
Boonville, CA 95415, United States
avbc.com

BANANA INVESTMENTS LIMITED

10123 Arusha, +255 Arusha, Tanzania
banana.co.tz

BALLAST POINT BREWING COMPANY

Miramar
9045 Carroll Way
San Diego, CA 92121, United States
ballastpoint.com

BELVOIR BREWERY

Crown Park, Station Road,
Old Dalby, Leicestershire, LE14 3NQ,
England
belvoirbrewery.co.uk

BORG BRUGGHÚS

Grjótháls 7-11
Reykjavík, Iceland
borgbrugghus.is

BREWDOG

Balmacassie Industrial Estate,
Ellon, Aberdeenshire, AB41 8BX
brewdog.com

BREWMEISTER

Isla Bank Mills,
Keith AB55 5DD, United Kingdom
craftbeerclanscotland.com

BROUWERIJ BOSTEELS

Kerkstraat 96, 9255 Buggenhout, Belgium
bestbelgianspecialbeers.be/en

BRUGGHUS STEDJA

Steðji Flókadal Borgarnes, Iceland 311
stedji.com/english.html

CHARLES WELLS BREWING

Havelock Street, Bedford, MK40 4LU
United Kingdom
charleswells.co.uk

DOCK STREET BREWERY

701 South 50th Street
Philadelphia, PA 19143
dockstreetbeer.com

DUPETIT

Hauptstraße 41, 63930 Neunkirchen,
Germany
dupetit.eu

EPIC BREWING COMPANY

Epic HQ
Unit 2, 761 Great South Rd
Penrose, Auckland, New Zealand
epicbeer.com

FLYING DOG BREWERY

4607 Wedgewood Blvd.
Frederick, MD 21703
flyingdogbrewery.com

GREAT LAKES BREWING COMPANY

2516 Market Ave, Cleveland, OH 44113,
United States
greatlakesbrewing.com

INDEPENDENCE BREWING COMPANY

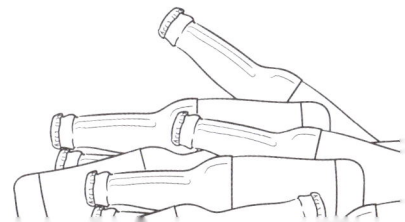

3913 Todd Lane Suite #607
Austin Texas 78744, United States
independencebrewing.com

JACK'S ABBEY CRAFT LAGERS
100 Clinton Street
Framingham, MA 01702, United States
jacksabby.com

JESTER KING BREWERY
Ceres Park, 13005 Fitzhugh Road
Austin, United States
jesterkingbrewery.com

LOST RHINO BREWING COMPANY
21730 Red Rum Drive, Suite 142
Ashburn, VA 20147, United States
lostrhino.com

MAMMA MIA! PIZZA BEER
mammamiapizzabeer.com

MATSO'S BROOME BREWERY
60 Hamersley St Broome, Western Australia
matsos.com.au

MERCHANT BREWING COMPANY
Marrickvile, Sydney, Australia
merchantbrewing.co

MIKKELLER
Mikkeller ApS, Vesterbrogade 20, 1.th.
DK-1620 Copenhagen V, Denmark
mikkeller.dk

MOON DOG CRAFT BREWERY
17 Duke Street
Abbotsford, Victoria, Australia
moondogbrewing.com.au

NAIL BREWING
4/301 Collier Road
Bassendean, Western Australia
nailbrewing.com.au

NEW BELGIUM BREWING COMPANY
500 Linden Street, Fort Collins, CO 80524
USA, United States
newbelgium.com

ODELL BREWING COMPANY
800 East Lincoln Ave Fort Collins, CO
80524, United States
odellbrewing.com

RED DUCK
11A Michaels Drive
Alfredton Ballarat Vic 3350, Australia
redduckbeer.com.au

RIGHT BRAIN BREWERY
225 East 16th Street, Traverse City, MI
49684, United States
rightbrainbrewery.com

ROGUE ALES
Rogue Ales Public House (one of many)
Newport, OR
748 SW Bay Blvd., Newport, OR, 97365
rogue.com

SANKT GALLEN BREWERY
Kaneda 1137-1
Kanagawa-ken Atsugi-shi, 243-0807, Japan
sanktgallenbrewery.com

SAPPORO
sapporoholdings.jp

SHORT'S BREWING COMPANY
121 N. Bridge St.
Bellaire, MI 49615, United States
shortsbrewing.com

SUNTORY
suntory.com

THE LOST ABBEY
155 Mata Way 104, San Marcos, CA 92069,
United States
lostabbey.com

TWO BIRDS BREWING
136 Hall Street, Spotswood,
Victoria 3015
twobirdsbrewing.com.au

WHEATY BREWING CORPS
39 George Street
Thebarton, Adelaide
wheatybrewingcorps.com

WILLIAM BROS. BREWING COMPANY
Kelliebank, New Alloa Brewery, Alloa
FK10 1NU, Scotland
williamsbrosbrew.com

WYNKOOP BREWING COMPANY
1634 18th St, Denver, CO 80202,
United States
wynkoop.com

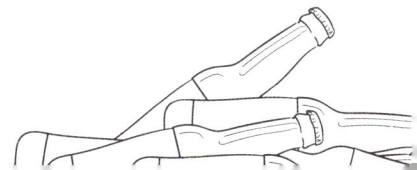

BREWED *with* BALLS

ACKNOWLEDGMENTS

A MASSIVE THANKS TO THE BREWERS AND BREWERIES featured in this book, without whom we wouldn't have much to talk about – we salute you! The creativity and gusto of this crowd is something to behold, and we thank them for their participation in this project and for their wider contribution to the human race.

Thanks also to the crew at Slow Beer for their assistance in selecting some pretty out-there brews that we at Affirm Press then consumed as 'research'. (Did we mention how good this book was to work on?)

A very special thanks to Josh Uljans, Karl van Buuren and all at Moon Dog brewery. Not only did they write an introduction for us, but they brewed us our very own Affirm Press beer! Legends.

And last but certainly not least, thanks to beer, the ballsiest beverage of them all.

PHOTO CREDITS